# Colors of Insects

by Laura Purdie Salas

CAPSTONE PRESS
a capstone imprint

More than half of all animal species on Earth are insects. Look at them closely. You'll see amazing things, like big, round eyes and glow-in-the-dark bellies! Sharp pincers, see-through wings, hairy legs, and glossy shells. And their colors are out of this world!

3

4

**Black** and **yellow** bumblebees have an important job. When they land on a flower, powdery pollen sticks to their feet. Bumblebees track the pollen from flower to flower. The pollen helps plants make new plants.

Shiny **purple** tiger beetles are small but fast. They are 0.5 inch (13 millimeters) long. They can run 54 times their body length in just one second! No person can run 54 times his body length in one second. Not even close!

Farmers love red and **black** ladybugs. These hungry beetles eat bugs that eat crops. Scientists believe their bright colors warn animals that ladybugs taste awful. Ladybugs also leak bad-tasting juice from their legs. Eeeww! What other bug would want to taste that?

The **brown** water scorpion is a true bug, not a scorpion. To breathe while swimming, it sticks its long, skinny snorkel up to the surface and takes in air. Water scorpions spear small fish and animals with their sharp front legs. Those legs are so sharp they can even stab human toes!

This **blue** morpho butterfly isn't really blue. Its wings have brown, not blue, pigment. But tiny scales on the wings reflect light. That makes the wings *look* blue. Armies are studying morpho butterflies. They hope to learn how to make better camouflage for soldiers.

Big **black** dung beetles eat one thing—poop. Dung is another word for poop. Most dung beetles shape brown dung into a large ball. Then they bury it for a tasty treat later. Some dung beetles can grow more than 6 inches (15 centimeters) long!

Guess which plant the lily beetle loves? That's right—lilies! This **red-orange** bug used to live only in Europe or northern Africa. It came to North America in the 1940s.

Have you ever seen a **pink** bug? Most long-winged katydids sport green bodies. But, surprise! Sometimes they are tan or pink. Katydids scrape their wings together to make music. Part of their bug song is too high-pitched for humans to hear.

What is this bug doing? Some people think it looks like it's praying. That's why it's called a praying mantis. It has a cool, green, leafy-looking body. That helps it hide while it hunts moths, grasshoppers, and other insects. It will even eat other praying mantids!

Monarch butterflies sport flashy **orange** and **black** wings. Those bright wings warn birds that monarchs taste icky. Monarchs fly south to Mexico and southern California every winter. They flutter up to 3,000 miles (4,828 kilometers). That's longer than any other butterfly migration!

Tiny **White**flies are only 1/16 inch (1.5 mm) long. In fact, 12 whiteflies could stand end-to-end across a single penny. But these tiny bugs can do lots of harm to plants. Little nibbles really add up!

This gorgeous **blue** damselfly looks a lot like a dragonfly. But see how its wings lie close to its body while it rests? A dragonfly's wings almost always stick out sideways.

This big, beautiful elephant hawk moth is **tan** and **pink**. Its wingspan is between 2.4 and 3 inches (60 and 75 mm). That's not quite as big as an elephant, but it's pretty big! This moth drinks flower nectar at night.

# Glossary

camouflage—coloring or clothing that makes something look like its surroundings

migration—the act of to traveling from one area to another on a regular basis

nectar—a sweet liquid found in many flowers

pigment—a substance that gives color to something

pincer—a body part that an animal uses to hold and pinch something

pollen—tiny yellow grains that flowers create to make new plants

scale—a hard, protective body covering for fish and reptiles

snorkel—a tube used when swimming underwater

species—a group of animals with similar features

true bug—a bug that has a hardened pair of wings and a mouth that is hard like a beak

# Read More

**Jackson, Cari.** *Bugs that Build.* Bug Alert. New York: Marshall Cavendish Benchmark, 2009.

**Markle, Sandra.** *Insects: Biggest! Littlest!* Honesdale, Pa.: Boyds Mills Press, 2009.

**Sutherland, Jonathan.** *Flying Insects.* Nature's Monsters: Insects & Spiders. Milwaukee: Gareth Stevens Pub., 2007.

# Internet Sites

FactHound offers a safe, fun way to find Internet sites related to this book. All of the sites on FactHound have been researched by our staff.

Here's all you do:

Visit www.facthound.com

Type in this code: 9781429652551

Check out projects, games and lots more at
www.capstonekids.com

A+ Books are published by Capstone Press,
151 Good Counsel Drive, P.O. Box 669, Mankato, Minnesota 56002.
www.capstonepub.com

Books published by Capstone Press are manufactured with paper
containing at least 10 percent post-consumer waste.

*Library of Congress Cataloging-in-Publication Data*
Salas, Laura Purdie.
  Colors of insects / by Laura Purdie Salas.
    p. cm.—(A+ books. colors all around)
  Includes bibliographical references and index.
  Summary: "Simple text and photographs illustrate the colors of insects"—Provided by publisher.
  ISBN 978-1-4296-5255-1 (library binding)
  ISBN 978-1-4296-6153-9 (paperback)
  1. Insects—Color—Juvenile literature.  I. Title.
  QL467.2.S25 2011
  595.7147'2—dc22                                    2010028173

**Credits**
Jenny Marks, editor; Bobbie Nuytten, designer; Svetlana Zhurkin, media researcher; Eric Manske,
    production specialist

**Photo Credits**
Alamy/John Quixley, 2–3; Papilio, 18–19; WildPictures, 24–25
Minden Pictures/FLPA/B. Borrell Casals, 10–11
Shutterstock/abxyz, 6–7; alexsmaga, 16–17; Alta Oosthuizen, 1; Becky Sheridan,
22–23; Cathy Keifer 26–27; Chekaramit, 28–29; Four Oaks, 14–15; Luna Vandoorne,
12–13; Robert Adrian Hillman (background), throughout; Stephen Inglis, 20–21;
Vladimir Sazonov, 4–5
Steve Marshall, cover, 6–7

**Note to Parents, Teachers, and Librarians**
The Colors All Around series supports national arts education standards related to identifying
colors in the environment. This book describes and illustrates colors seen in insects. The images
support early readers in understanding the text. The repetition of words and phrases helps early
readers learn new words. This book also introduces early readers to subject-specific vocabulary
words, which are defined in the Glossary section. Early readers may need assistance to read some
words and to use the Table of Contents, Glossary, Read More, Internet Sites, and Index sections
of the book.

Printed in the United States of America in North Mankato, Minnesota.
092010      005933CGS11

ML                                    6/11